Animals
on the
Edge

**Science Races
to Save Species
Threatened With
Extinction**

Animals
on the
Edge

Science Races to Save Species
Threatened With Extinction

By Sandra Pobst
Todd K. Fuller, Consultant

NATIONAL
GEOGRAPHIC
Washington, D.C.

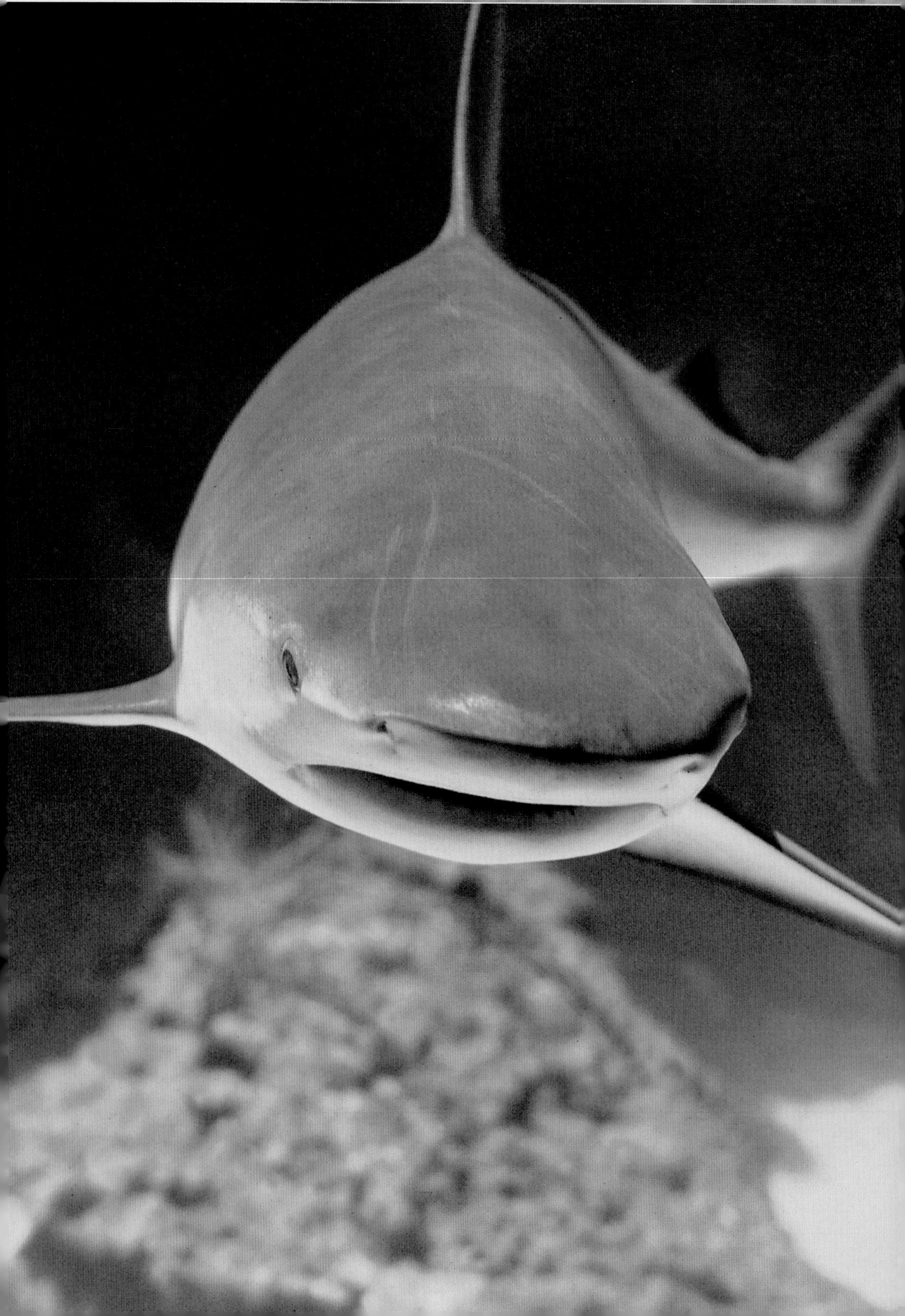

Contents

◁ The Census of Marine Life will give scientists a better idea of the numbers of fish, plant life, and marine mammals throughout the world's oceans. Keeping track of populations of endangered species like the great white shark, pictured here, will become easier.

◁ St. Paul Island, Alaska, is home to millions of seabirds that nest along the ledges of its steep cliffs. Some species found on the island do not breed anywhere else in the world. Oil spills and invasive species like rats and foxes threaten these bird populations.

From the Consultant

When I first visited East Africa 22 years ago, I couldn't believe how many animals—and how many different kinds of animals—I saw. But one fellow I met who had come to Africa 10 years before I did said that if I thought what I saw was spectacular, I should have seen it when he arrived—things were so much better. Then he paused, looked kind of sad, and said that an African old-timer had said the same thing to him when he had arrived, and now he wondered where it was all going to end up.

The world has been changing rapidly, even in the places we think are treasures and trust will be around forever. The people described in this book, and many others, are devoting their lives to trying to save the species and ecosystems we have left. You'll see that

there are many different ways to find out how things work and what kinds of actions might be taken to conserve plants and animals and the landscapes they live in. If things seem in urgent need of help, it's true. There is no tomorrow when it comes to making up for all of the mistakes we've made, and by understanding what needs to be done, you can make a difference and help the world remain the true wonderland that it's supposed to be.

Todd K. Fuller
Massachusetts, 2008

∧ Although domesticated Bactrian camels (like this one) are common throughout Central Asia, the entire population of wild individuals lives in the Gobi Desert and numbers less than 1,000.

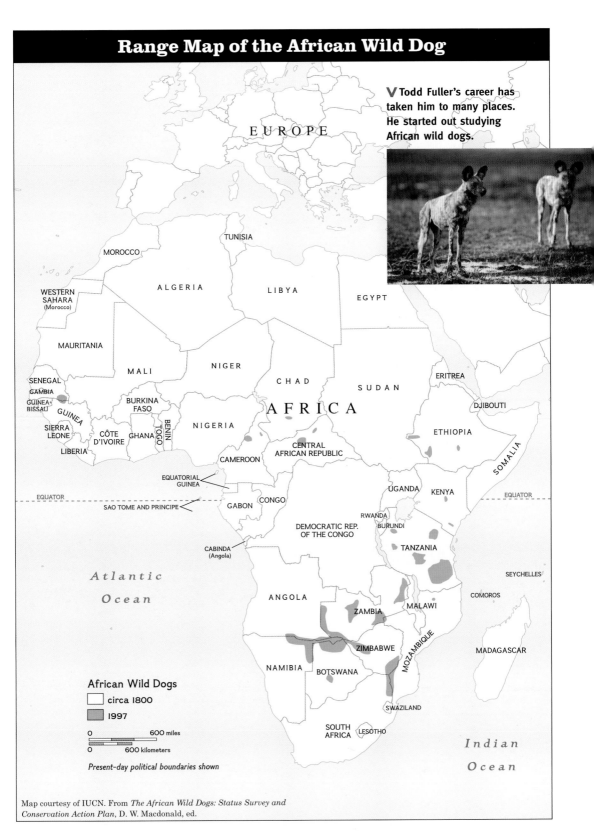

Range Map of the African Wild Dog

▼ Todd Fuller's career has taken him to many places. He started out studying African wild dogs.

EUROPE

AFRICA

TUNISIA
MOROCCO
WESTERN SAHARA (Morocco)
ALGERIA
LIBYA
EGYPT
MAURITANIA
MALI
NIGER
CHAD
SUDAN
ERITREA
SENEGAL
GAMBIA
GUINEA-BISSAU
GUINEA
BURKINA FASO
BENIN
TOGO
NIGERIA
DJIBOUTI
SIERRA LEONE
CÔTE D'IVOIRE
GHANA
LIBERIA
CAMEROON
CENTRAL AFRICAN REPUBLIC
ETHIOPIA
SOMALIA
EQUATORIAL GUINEA
SAO TOME AND PRINCIPE
GABON
CONGO
UGANDA
KENYA
DEMOCRATIC REP. OF THE CONGO
RWANDA
BURUNDI
CABINDA (Angola)
TANZANIA
SEYCHELLES
COMOROS
ANGOLA
ZAMBIA
MALAWI
MOZAMBIQUE
MADAGASCAR
ZIMBABWE
NAMIBIA
BOTSWANA
SWAZILAND
SOUTH AFRICA
LESOTHO

EQUATOR

Atlantic Ocean

Indian Ocean

African Wild Dogs

☐ circa 1800
▨ 1997

0   600 miles
0   600 kilometers

Present-day political boundaries shown

Map courtesy of IUCN. From *The African Wild Dogs: Status Survey and Conservation Action Plan*, D. W. Macdonald, ed.

TIMELINE OF
Animal Conservation Events

< **1944** · Once on the brink of extinction, whooping crane populations have been revitalized since the 1950s. Still, only three flocks totaling 336 birds remain in the wild today.

> **1969** · Estimates put the humpback whale population at approximately 1,000 throughout the world, down from 200,000 in the mid-20th century.

| 1900 | 1920 | 1940 | 1960 | 1970 |

1914

The passenger pigeon, once the most numerous bird on Earth, becomes extinct.

1916

Congress creates the National Park Service and National Park System protecting the habitat of hundreds of species around the nation.

1944

Only 21 whooping cranes remain in the wild.

1969

Greenpeace is founded to protest whale hunting and nuclear testing.

1972

DDT, a pesticide responsible for declining bird populations, is banned in the United States. Congress passes the Marine Mammal Protection Act to protect polar bears, whales, dolphins, and other marine mammals.

1966

Congress passes the first Endangered Species Act, though it provides little protection for the animals listed as endangered.

< **1994** · The bald eagle moves from endangered to threatened. Bald eagles can now be found in every U.S. state except Hawaii.

< **1972** · DDT, used to prevent livestock from insects and insect-borne disease, and as a pesticide on crops, had disastrous effects on bird populations before it was banned.

V **2000** · California condors, bred in captivity and released into the wild, carry blue tags so Fish and Wildlife officials can monitor their progress and population recovery.

∧ **1980** · Jimmy Carter holds up a copy of the Alaska land bill he signed into law, placing more than 100 million acres of Alaskan wilderness under government protection.

1980   1990   2000

1973

Congress passes the second Endangered Species Act, requiring the government to protect the habitat of listed plants and animals as well as the species themselves.

1980s

The Alaska National Interest Lands Conservation Act establishes new national parks, wildlife refuges, and national forests.

The few remaining wild California condors, red wolves, and black-footed ferrets are captured to begin captive breeding programs.

1994

The bald eagle population grows, updating its status from endangered to threatened.

1991

Black-footed ferrets bred in captivity are reintroduced into the wild in Wyoming.

1997

The National Wildlife Refuge System Improvement Act strengthens the protection of wildlife and conservation of habitat in America's national wildlife refuges.

2000

A pair of released captive-bred California condors successfully breed in the wild. It is the first time condors have bred in their natural habitat in 18 years.

Animals in Danger

CHAPTER 1

On the Brink of Extinction

A helicopter thunders over the frozen landscape of Canada's Northwest Territories. Below, a polar bear runs from the noise. The door of the helicopter opens. A man leans out, aims a gun at the bear, and shoots a tranquilizing dart. The bear continues running for a few minutes, then finally misses a step and falls to the ground. The helicopter lands nearby, and two polar bear researchers climb out.

It's April, and the darkness of winter has been replaced by 18-hour days here, north of the Arctic Circle. Temperatures have warmed up, too, reaching

< There are nearly 1,000 polar bears living in Manitoba, Canada, but weights and reproductive rates have declined in the last decade.

6°F (−14°C) at midday. The researchers watch the creamy-white bear carefully to make sure it is asleep before they approach. Male polar bears can weigh as much as 1,700 pounds (770 kg) and reach five feet (1.6 m) at the shoulder. Females are smaller, but still twice the size of a man. Researchers carry rifles or handguns for protection, since the powerful bears can be unpredictable if they wake too soon.

The tranquilized bear will sleep for only a few hours, so the scientists must work quickly. One researcher opens the bear's mouth and pulls a small tooth. It will be used to determine the age of the young female bear. The other researcher takes blood and blubber samples. The two men work together to measure the bear and estimate its weight. A microchip is injected below the bear's skin. The chip will help scientists identify this bear and track its health over time. Then a radio collar is fastened around the bear's neck. The collar allows scientists to track the bear's movements from a distant location. Finally, a number is painted on the bear's rump. When researchers spot this bear from the air, they will know it has already been captured and tested this year. As soon as they are finished gathering samples, the scientists pack up their equipment and return to the helicopter.

> Great apes face extinction in Africa.

Nowhere to Hide

Thousands of animal species around the world are in danger of disappearing forever. These animals are known as endangered species.

Many of these animals are endangered because they have lost their habitat. Great apes in Indonesia and Africa hover on the brink of extinction while the rain

forests they live in continue to be cleared for mining and farming. Roads and housing developments now surround the few remaining Florida panthers, animals that once roamed the southeastern United States. Animals are also harmed by pollution. Oil spills smother some marine animals, like seabirds. Chemicals such as PCBs and DDT, now banned from use, have been found at high levels in orcas and other marine animals as well as land animals. Trash can be just as deadly, choking or strangling animals like sea turtles that mistake garbage for food. Overhunting and overfishing have caused serious decreases in many animal populations. In some countries, people depend upon wild animals for food. However, so many are killed that the population is unable to recover. Sometimes animals are hunted illegally because there is a demand for their parts on the black market. In many cultures, people believe that adding tiger bones or rhino horns to traditional medicines will cure diseases. Poachers can get paid as much as $50,000 for a single tiger.

Weather changes due to global warming also affect many species. As average temperatures rise, the habitats of animals may change. If the animals cannot adapt quickly enough or move to a cooler environment, they may die. Polar bears and other Arctic animals in

∧ Fewer than 50 Florida panthers remain in the wild. The Florida Panther National Wildlife Refuge was established on more than 26,000 acres (10,530 ha) in Collier County, Florida, in 1989 to protect this subspecies of mountain lion.

particular are affected by changes in the ice cap due to Earth's warming temperatures. Polar bear populations in western Hudson Bay in Canada have been decreasing since 1987. Early ice melts leave the bears less time to hunt seals and build up blubber. Fewer survive the summer fasting period, and those that do survive are smaller and weaker.

Protecting Animals

In 1914, Americans were shocked when the last passenger pigeon died. Only fifty years earlier, giant flocks of over a billion birds had darkened the sky for hours as they flew by.

> Passenger pigeons, probably once the most numerous birds on earth, were driven to extinction by 1914 through overhunting.

15

People noticed that other animals that had once been plentiful, like buffalo and whooping cranes, were rarely seen. Over the next few decades, Americans began speaking up in favor of protecting wildlife.

In 1973, the United States passed the second Endangered Species Act (ESA). This law protects many plants and animals around the world that are at risk of becoming extinct. Animals and plants protected by the law are listed as either "threatened" or "endangered." An endangered species is in danger of becoming extinct in all or part of its habitat. A threatened species is likely to become endangered in the near future. The ESA makes it a crime to do anything that results in the death of an animal on the list. The law protects the habitat where the animal lives. The law also requires the government to conserve, or try to increase the populations of, endangered species.

Currently, almost 1,300 species are protected under the ESA. These protections have helped save peregrine falcons, gray whales, and sea otters, among other animals, from extinction.

∧ An Ethiopian police officer looks over a stash of illegal wildlife products seized in a 2005 raid on more than 60 shops in the capital city of Addis Ababa. Carved ivory, stuffed animals, and ostrich eggs were among the 1,100 pounds (500 kg) of illegal goods collected.

Global Warming

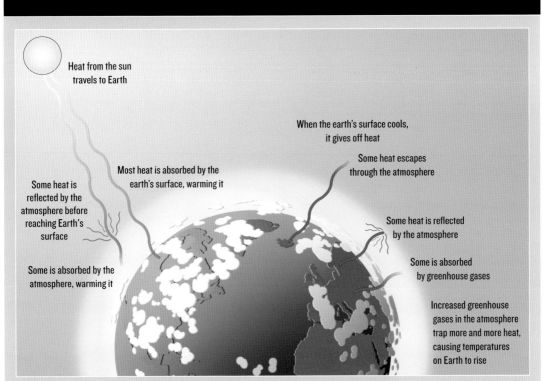

Heat from the sun travels to Earth

When the earth's surface cools, it gives off heat

Some heat escapes through the atmosphere

Most heat is absorbed by the earth's surface, warming it

Some heat is reflected by the atmosphere before reaching Earth's surface

Some heat is reflected by the atmosphere

Some is absorbed by the atmosphere, warming it

Some is absorbed by greenhouse gases

Increased greenhouse gases in the atmosphere trap more and more heat, causing temperatures on Earth to rise

Global warming has been blamed for record-breaking heat waves, droughts, melting polar ice, and increased flooding in coastal areas. Plants and animals that cannot adapt quickly enough to climate changes face extinction. But what is global warming?

Earth is surrounded by a layer of gases called the atmosphere. Some of these gases, such as carbon monoxide and methane, trap the sun's heat. This is known as the greenhouse effect. Without the warmth of this protective atmosphere, surface temperatures in much of the world would rarely be above freezing.

Since the Industrial Revolution in the 18th century, however, the mixture of gases in the atmosphere has been changing. Burning fossil fuels (coal, natural gas, and gasoline) to generate electricity and to power factories and cars has increased the amount of carbon dioxide in the atmosphere. So has the widespread cutting of forests around the world, diminishing the number of trees which absorb carbon dioxide. Ever-increasing amounts of trash dumped in landfills produce larger amounts of methane. All of that extra carbon dioxide and methane traps more of the sun's heat, causing temperatures on Earth to rise.

Climate changes naturally over time. For example, a gradual warming melted the ice sheets that once covered much of North America and Europe. Those changes, however, occurred over thousands of years. Today, average temperatures are about 1°F (0.56°C) higher than they were 100 years ago. That does not seem like much, but even a small change in average temperature has had a big impact. Ice sheets and glaciers are melting. Ocean levels are rising and desert areas are increasing.

∧ The Western North Carolina Nature Center in Asheville, North Carolina, is home to Wilson, an adult male red wolf. The center manages a captive breeding program established by the U.S. Fish and Wildlife Service in 1973.

Why Worry About Animals?

Some people wonder why we should make the effort to save animals that are in danger of becoming extinct. After all, species have been going extinct throughout history as natural conditions changed.

The changes occurring today, however, are primarily the result of human activity. As the world's population has grown, forests have been cut down, prairies plowed under for farms, cities have expanded, and factories and cars have spewed pollution into the air and water. Illegal killing of animals has also increased as some cultures highly value products made from protected animals. Our activities are threatening the existence of many animals; therefore, it is our responsibility to protect those that remain. Additionally, the impact of one species' extinction cannot be predicted. Living organisms within an ecosystem have very complex relationships. Subtracting one kind of plant or animal is certain to affect many others.

Many of today's medicines come directly from plants and animals. A fungus gave us penicillin, the first antibiotic. Effective cancer drugs have been developed from chemicals produced by some endangered Caribbean sea sponges. Other plants and animals are certain to hold chemical secrets yet undiscovered.

For many people, the amazing beauty of animals in the wild is reason enough to protect them. Never again seeing a grizzly in the forests of Yellowstone or hearing the mournful howl of red wolves echoing over a meadow would erase a vital part of our heritage, diminishing us all.

Historically, the world lost one species to extinction every century. Today, an estimated 20 to 40 species become extinct every day. In an effort to save these animals, scientists are combining new technology with proven conservation measures. In the chapters that follow, you will meet some of these extraordinary men and women and learn more about the science that supports and protects endangered species.

Λ Tony Dills, an animal curator at the Western North Carolina Nature Center, examines one of five wolf pups fathered by Wilson.

V The Rachel Carson National Wildlife Refuge was established in Maine in 1966 to protect wetlands where migratory birds nest.

Counting Heads (and Tails)

CHAPTER 2

Keeping Track of Animal Populations

Danny Stone and Carson pause for a minute in the Douglas firs that shade a slope of the Cascade Mountains in Washington State. Sunlight filters through the dense forest, punctuating the pine needles that carpet the ground. Carson is eager to get to work, and Danny soon issues the command Carson is waiting to hear: "Go find it!"

Carson, a yellow Labrador retriever, responds immediately to his handler's voice. He bounds through the towering trees, pausing from time to time to sniff the air. A silver bell is attached to

< Carson, a yellow Labrador retriever, scrambles over fallen trees on the forest floor, looking for evidence that grizzly bears are living in the Wenatchee National Forest in Washington State.

Carson's bright red harness. Its constant jingle warns bears and other wild animals of his presence.

Suddenly, something catches Carson's attention. His tail beats frantically as he dashes back and forth over an increasingly smaller area. Then, abruptly, he sits and waits for Danny to catch up. He has found what he has been looking for: a pile of bear scat, or poop.

While Carson accepts Danny's praise, Meg Decker, a scientist working for the U.S. Forest Service, records information about the scat. She notes the location of the scat, determines what the bear has been eating, and estimates how old the scat is. Then she preserves a small sample for DNA testing.

When the bear scat reaches Dr. Samuel Wasser's laboratory at the University of Washington, it is thoroughly analyzed. The scat contains DNA (a genetic map) and hormones that provide useful information about the animal that left it. After analyzing the scat in the lab, scientists will know whether the animal is a black bear or a grizzly, male or female. They will have a picture of the bear's health and stress levels. Most importantly, all this information can be gathered without ever confronting the animal.

∧ **Meg Decker, a scientist with the U.S. Forest Service, investigates a piece of bear scat that Carson (in the left background with his handler) has found.**

∧ About 500 grizzly bears currently live in the areas of Idaho, Montana, and Wyoming that make up Yellowstone National Park.

Canines for Conservation

Dr. Wasser, director of the University of Washington's Center for Conservation Biology, pioneered the use of scat detection dogs in 1997. Four dogs and their handlers searched nearly 2,000 square miles (5,000 sq km) three times at two-week intervals and found hundreds of scat samples. This has proved to be more efficient and less expensive than many other methods used for counting animal populations in the wild.

On this search, wildlife biologists used Carson and three other dogs to scour 100 square miles (260 sq km) in the Cascades for proof that grizzly bears still live there. (It is estimated that fewer than 20 grizzlies still live in the northern Cascades.) If some of the 250 scat samples found by the dogs are from grizzlies, scientists will have a better idea of where the threatened bears are living. Months later, when all the material was analyzed, Dr. Wasser's team was successful in finding evidence of grizzlies in the region.

The Census Counts

One of the biggest challenges facing biologists working with endangered species is counting how many animals are living in a particular area. It is important, though, because comparing the number of animals over time shows whether a population is increasing or decreasing.

Getting an accurate count—called a survey—of an animal population in the wild is tricky at best. Actually counting every animal in an area is usually impossible. As a result, wildlife biologists have developed a variety of methods to estimate the population of a species. Scientists choose a survey method based on the movement patterns of the animal population, the accuracy that is required, and the amount of data that are needed.

Barcode of Life

∧ **High Tech High students are assisting the San Diego Zoo in efforts to genetically identify products made from endangered species.**

An international project called the Consortium for the Barcode of Life (CBOL) is creating a library that will eventually contain the DNA sequences for all known animals and plants on Earth.

Scientists from museums, zoos, universities, private industry, and other organizations are working together to obtain DNA samples of known animals. The DNA sequence for each species is represented by a barcode, similar to those read by scanners at stores. The barcodes are then stored in a public database.

The barcodes can be used to determine the source of animal products. In 2006, students at High Tech High in San Diego worked with the San Diego Zoo's Center for Conservation and Research for Endangered Species on a research project to show that DNA could be extracted from jerky (dried meat). The resulting DNA barcodes were compared to those stored in the CBOL database to determine the type of meat used to make the jerky. The students successfully identified ostrich, beef, and turkey meat.

The students' success launched a new project. In it, they will try to identify the source of dried meats from Africa that have been seized by U.S. Customs officials. Using the processes that they pioneered, the students will determine whether any of the products contain bushmeat from endangered species such as chimpanzees or gorillas. Selling bushmeat obviously threatens endangered species. In addition, the meat often carries diseases, including the Ebola virus or monkeypox, which can be deadly to humans.

Tracking Them Down

Some survey methods require direct interaction between animals and humans. For instance, animals may be caught in traps baited with food or tranquilized and marked with ear tags or some other identifying mark. They are then released. Scientists track how many animals are captured during each survey and note how many of the marked animals are recaptured later. Using this information, they can estimate the population of the species. This method is not always reliable, however, since some animals that have been trapped once avoid the traps later. Other animals keep returning to the traps, hoping for another food reward. In addition, the stress caused by being trapped can cause health problems in a population that is already at risk.

∧ Methods for tracking tigers in India include using digitized images of tiger pugs (paw prints) to identify individual cats. Field workers make casts of paw prints found in the wild and bring them back to the lab where pictures are taken of them and added to a database. There are probably fewer than 3,000 tigers left in India.

Other survey methods avoid contact with animals. Instead, teams of scientists and volunteers systematically search for evidence—such as tracks, dens, feeding sites, or scat—of the animals being counted. This method avoids stressing the animals, but such surveys can be time-consuming and expensive. For instance, a recent census of China's giant panda population took four years to complete and involved nearly 200 people. The method can also be dangerous. During a recent tiger census in the Indian delta, 450 people were outfitted with fiberglass protective vests. Armed guards protected the teams while they made plaster molds of tiger prints, and medical workers were present in case of a tiger attack.

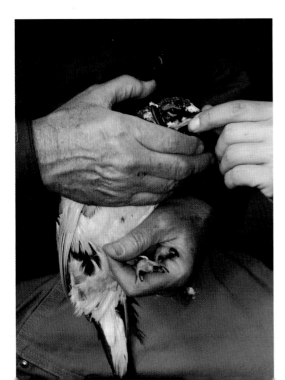

< An Evermann's rock ptarmigan is outfitted with a radio harness for tracking purposes. This arctic bird is recognized as a species of special management concern by the U.S. Fish and Wildlife Service, which is hoping to restore the ptarmigan population in southwestern Alaska.

Sea Survey

We can name many of the animals that live in the world's oceans, but we often know little about their habits and the environment they live in. For instance, do whale sharks migrate? What organisms live under the Arctic ice cap? How do loggerhead sea turtles interact with other species?

To answer these questions and more, a group of marine scientists met in 2000 to design the Census of Marine Life. This ambitious ten-year project involves more than 1,700 scientists from over 70 countries. Teams of researchers are actively exploring the diversity of life in each ocean ecosystem, from shallow tidal zones to deep trenches to undersea mountains.

Until recently, scientists did not have the tools that they needed to conduct this type of survey. One important breakthrough was the development of small, yet powerful data collection tags which attach to an animal. Scientists set the tags to record data at specific time intervals, which vary depending upon the species. They also specify how long the tags will remain attached, up to a year.

Once attached, the tag periodically records the location of the animal. It also records the ocean depth, temperature, amount of light, and other information. After the specified time period, the tag pops off the animal and floats to the ocean's surface. There, it transmits the data to the researchers via satellite. Other scientists are using remote-controlled underwater vehicles, special cameras, and divers to gather information.

When the survey ends in 2010, we will have a clearer understanding of historic marine populations. This data will help scientists predict how ocean life may change in the future.

▽ Oceanographer Dr. Sylvia Earle, left, and an unidentified diver examine fish reference charts In the Florida Keys National Marine Sanctuary.

Λ Staff at Virachey National Park in Cambodia attach a camera trap to a tree in order to record the presence of elephants and tigers in the preserve.

Smile!

Survey methods such as camera trapping avoid human-animal interaction altogether. Here, cameras are enclosed in weatherproof cases and secured to trees near wildlife trails. When an animal moves along the trail, a motion sensor triggers the camera to take a photograph. Depending upon the size of the area being surveyed, hundreds of cameras might be set up.

Camera traps can be quite useful when counting populations of nocturnal animals as well as animals that live in remote areas. Over time, the photographs help scientists determine the species that live in a particular area, their populations, and their activity patterns.

If You Cannot Look, Listen

Biologists have always been interested in the sounds that animals make to communicate. Now scientists at the Bioacoustics Research Program at Cornell University have developed a way to use those sounds to count animal populations. Special computer software translates recorded animal calls into a spectrogram, a visual image of a sound. This allows scientists to measure and analyze the sounds different animals make. Scientists are using bioacoustics as a survey method for animals that are hard to see, such as birds, whales, and forest elephants.

Cornell's Elephant Listening Project focuses on the African forest elephants. These elephants, identified as a separate species in 2001, live deep in the central African forests and are rarely seen. Researchers set up recorders to capture the calls of the elephants. By analyzing the rate at which elephants call to each other, scientists are able to estimate the population of a herd. Recordings have also alerted researchers and authorities to gunshots and vehicles, possible signs of poachers in the area.

Λ The field of bioacoustics has helped researchers estimate the number of elephants living in a region, even when those elephants can't be seen.

The Law Is on Their Side

CHAPTER 3

Crimes Against Endangered Animals

In a hotel room in Japan, two scientists carefully unpack their equipment and set up a temporary lab. Before long, an off-duty wildlife officer arrives, delivering sixteen packages for testing. Each package holds a piece of whale meat, purchased legally at fish markets throughout Japan. When the scientists finish their testing, however, they will know whether the whale meat comes from the minke whales that can be sold legally in Japan or from endangered whales.

Dr. Stephen R. Palumbi, a marine biologist, and Dr. Scott Baker, a molecular ecologist, prepare

< A female humpback whale and her calf swim in the waters of the Kingdom of Tonga, an island nation in the Pacific. Once up to 10,000 whales migrated to this region, but the population is now less than 500.

∧ Whale meat is displayed for shoppers in a market in Tokyo, Japan. Environmental groups in the United States have succeeded in persuading some of Japan's longtime whaling companies to end sales of whale meat.

samples of each piece of whale meat. The samples are then run through a thermal cycler. This small machine extracts the DNA from the tissue, then copies the DNA millions of times. This ability to make copies is important for the scientists conducting these tests. If the whale meat proves to be from endangered species, it would be illegal for them to transport the meat out of the country. The scientists could take the copies of the DNA, however, and analyze them more thoroughly in their own labs back in the United

States. More than half the samples turn out to be southern minke. Five of the sixteen samples come from species that are protected, including the humpback whale. Some samples come from dolphins, while others come from other types of whales.

The presence of the meat from endangered whales in the markets does not mean that Japanese whalers killed the whales. Whalers around the world sell whale meat— from any whale—to Japan, where it is considered a delicacy. The test results do show, however, that more needs to be done to prevent the harvest and sale of products from endangered whales.

A DNA registry could provide proof that whales have been legally caught. A DNA registry is a database that would genetically identify all whales taken for commercial or scientific purposes and make that information available to a monitoring body. However, Japan and Norway—the two countries that continue commercial and research whaling—have resisted efforts to have independent observers check their whale stock. More troubling was the news in 2005 that Japan was expanding its whaling research program. Among the whales that were targeted for capture were humpback, fin, and sei whales, all of which are protected species.

DNA Detectives

Since the late 1980s, DNA testing has proved effective in tracking down and arresting criminals. Now it is being used to track down poachers and others who prey on endangered wildlife.

In 2002, officials in Singapore seized 6.5 tons (5.9 metric tons) of illegal elephant ivory. The shipment included more than 500 whole tusks, many over 6 feet (2 m) long. Over 40,000 thumb-sized ivory signature seals, valued at more than $8 million, made up the rest of the shipment. International police investigators

∧ A bull elephant's ivory tusks can bring thousands of dollars to traders on the black market. New DNA techniques enable scientists to trace ivory back to its country of origin.

∨ This shipment of 6.5 tons (5.9 metric tons) of ivory originated in Zambia, was seized in Singapore, and was due to ship to Japan, where there is a large demand for illegal ivory.

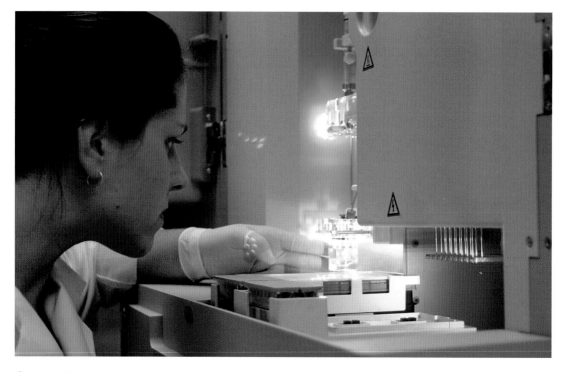

∧ A scientist analyzes DNA taken from samples of goods seized in raids on illegal wildlife products. In order to catch wildlife criminals, hair, bone, tusks, and blood are all used to analyze where animals and their by-products come from.

tracked the shipment back to Zambia, a country in southern Africa. But they had no way of telling whether the elephants had been killed there. One of the officers knew that Samuel Wasser, the conservation biologist at the University of Washington, had been compiling a map of elephant DNA. Wasser and his colleagues had collected elephant dung from 23 African countries. After extracting and comparing the DNA, researchers discovered that they could identify where an elephant lived based on its DNA.

Obviously, this DNA map could help Interpol (the International Criminal Police Organization) track down the origin of the ivory. But first Wasser had to figure out how to get DNA samples out of the ivory. Grinding off small samples created too much heat and destroyed the DNA. So Wasser talked with dentists to find out how they acquired DNA from teeth. He discovered that freezing the ivory and then pulverizing it created a fine powder that retained its DNA. When the DNA was analyzed and compared to the compiled DNA map, Wasser's team found that all the ivory came from Zambia. This information allows law enforcement groups to focus their efforts in that region and forces Zambia to take responsibility for the intensive poaching within its borders.

Looking Out for Bears

The use of DNA analysis to prove crimes against endangered animals is on the rise. The tests can be lengthy and expensive, however. In 2007, a different kind of DNA test was developed to help in the fight against wildlife crime. It targets traditional Asian medicines, which often include tissues or organs from protected animals, especially bears. While bears are legally raised on farms in China, Korea, and Vietnam, laws restrict the international sales of products from bears. Despite the laws, there is a growing market outside of Asia for traditional medicines containing bear bile.

Officials involved with animal protection groups are particularly concerned about the inhumane way bears are raised and treated on these farms. The animals are housed in cramped quarters. To remove bile from the live bears, the bear is fitted with an intravenous tube that extracts bile from the gall bladder. It is painful and bears often die from infections associated with the wound site.

With the new test, customs officials and wildlife officers can check suspected materials immediately. A sample of the medicine is mixed with a liquid chemical. Then a test strip is dipped into the mixture. If any protein from bears is in the mixture, a double blue line appears on the test strip within five minutes. This test enables officials to immediately seize the products and track down the exporters who are selling the medicines illegally.

▼ DNA testing is helping to prevent the illegal sale of products containing bear parts. It is hoped that cracking down on the illegal trafficking of these items will make bear farming in Asia a less profitable business. Thousands of bears are raised in inhumane conditions on bear farms throughout China, Vietnam, and South Korea.

Meet a Conservation Biologist

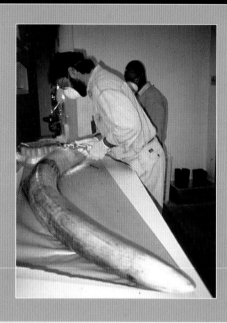

Dr. Samuel K. Wasser, director of the University of Washington's Center for Conservation Biology, is a leader in developing new techniques to monitor the health and population of endangered and threatened species without disturbing the animals.

How did you become interested in conservation biology (the study and protection of Earth's biological diversity)?

When I was in college, I was studying animal behavior. I had the opportunity to go to Uganda to participate in field research. But when I arrived in Kenya, I found a note saying that the study was scrapped. Idi Amin's army had destroyed the camp and the researcher was in hiding. I got permission to do my own study on lions, looking at how their social behavior changed as their prey migrated. That got me hooked on evolutionary biology (the study of how a species changes over time).

Then, in 1979, I went back to Africa, to the Mikumi-Selous protected area in Tanzania to study baboons and how females regulate their fertility cycles. I wanted to measure the stress and reproductive hormones of each animal and found that I could do that by testing their feces.

I was in Tanzania through the 1980s. I saw the long-term impact of poaching on elephant herds, how long it took them to recover, and how the groups functioned when members had been slaughtered. I knew I had to get involved in conservation.

You were among the pioneers who successfully extracted DNA from feces. How difficult was that process?

I had been working on hormones for ten years, so I had lots of experience. It was a matter of persistence. You just keep experimenting, trying a variety of methods; eventually you find the one that works best.

Your work with scat detection dogs has gathered a lot of interest. What gave you the idea to use dogs to locate whale poop?

The New England Aquarium had been sending us samples of right whale poop for hormone analysis. Now, right whale poop is bright orange. It floats, and it stinks. But after several days on the boat, I noticed that [the scientists] often couldn't find it in the choppy water. I thought this is absolutely perfect for dogs. With the wind blowing across the water, the dogs should have no trouble finding it. And we were right!

What is a typical day like for you?

It's really quite varied. I don't spend as much time in the field as in the past. I used to spend a year in Africa and a year out. Now, I'm driving the projects rather than doing the actual lab or field work. I usually spend a couple of weeks in the field when a new project begins. I also work with graduate and post-doc students here at the university.

Raising money takes a lot of my time. We have to get grants to fund our research. Talking with the media takes an increasing amount of time, too. People are always interested in the detection dog program. Because of that, we have a great opportunity to make people more aware of conservation problems.

Lately, I've spent more time working with governments

∧ **A lab technician works with frozen DNA that may yield results that can lead to convictions for wildlife crimes.**

and law enforcement agencies, developing wildlife forensics programs (scientific procedures used to analyze evidence from crime scenes associated with the illegal killing of animals or sale of products from protected species).

What do you think it's important for kids to know about endangered species?

I wish everyone could see how wonderful animals are. They have unique needs, and they don't have a lot of options when their habitat disappears. The more unique the animal is, the less likely it is to recover once it's threatened.

People impact wildlife by their behavior every day. We tend to use a lot of resources in the United States. Everyone wants the latest thing—cell phone, video game—even if they have one that still works. Manufacturing new electronics and other things uses up resources and creates pollution. The things that are thrown away fill up landfills. If it were just one person, that might not make a big difference. But when everyone does it, it's huge!

Helping Mother Nature

CHAPTER 4

Breeding Animals in Captivity

The medical team gathers around the operating table in the brightly lit, sterile operating room. Bluebelle, a female black-footed ferret, lies anesthetized on the table. Her belly has been shaved and scrubbed with antiseptic. A video monitor is located at the end of the table.

Dr. JoGayle Howard makes a small incision in the ferret's abdomen. Then she carefully inserts a laparoscope, a slender metal tool, through the cut. A camera on the end of the laparoscope sends pictures of the ferret's inner organs to the video monitor. Watching the monitor, Dr. Howard quickly locates

< Captive breeding programs for the black-footed ferret have been responsible for the birth of approximately 300 kits (baby ferrets) a year. Approximately 1/3 of the animals born each year are kept in captivity to continue the program.

the uterus and proceeds to artificially inseminate the ferret. She guides a thin, hollow needle into the uterus and positions it near an ovary. A solution containing semen is injected through the needle. After repeating the procedure near the other ovary, the needles and laparoscope are removed, and Bluebelle is on her way to the recovery room.

Seven weeks later, Bluebelle delivers five healthy kits.

Captive Breeding Programs

The National Zoo's Conservation and Research Center in Front Royal, Virginia, is a leader in the race to rescue black-footed ferrets from extinction. When the animals were threatened by disease in 1987, biologists captured the remaining 18 wild ferrets. These ferrets were placed in captive breeding programs such as the one at the National Zoo. Captive breeding programs are mating programs designed for use with animals in captivity. Today, the black-footed ferret population has risen to 1,000.

Survival School

Captive breeding programs are just the first step in increasing the population of a species. The ultimate goal is to reintroduce the animals to the wild and establish a self-sustaining population there. In many cases, the babies must first be taught how to survive in the wild.

At the National Zoo and other captive breeding sites, prairie dogs are brought in to create burrows in large pens. The prairie dogs are then removed, and a mother ferret and her kits move in. There, the kits adjust to living in a burrow. Eventually, prairie dogs are reintroduced. After demonstrating that they can kill prairie dogs for food, the ferrets are ready to be released into the wild.

Other species have also been saved from extinction by captive breeding programs. Among them are the golden lion tamarin, a Brazilian monkey; the scimitar-horned oryx, a kind of antelope; and the California condor.

V **The golden lion tamarin, a small squirrel-sized monkey native to Brazil, is endangered due to destruction of its habitat. About a thousand tamarins have been released into the wild, the result of successful captive breeding programs.**

Conservationists have high hopes for the reemergence of the California condor, a species that was listed as endangered in 1967.

Improving the Gene Pool

When a species' population dwindles to a critical level and there are few breeding individuals left, the animals that are reproducing are usually related to each other. As a result, inbreeding occurs. This means that the variety of genetic material that is passed along to future generations is limited. This lack of genetic diversity causes serious problems for already endangered species. Offspring may be infertile or have reduced resistance to disease.

To offset this loss of genetic diversity, many zoos and research centers are collecting genetic material—tissue, eggs, embryos, and sperm—from threatened and endangered species. Cells from hundreds of animals—including tigers, pandas, condors, and gray whales—are stored in gene banks, often called "frozen zoos." Cell tissue stored in the frozen zoo can be used in a variety of assisted reproductive techniques. Sperm is sometimes used for artificial insemination, as with the black-footed ferrets. In other cases, eggs and sperm are combined outside the animal's body in a process called in vitro fertilization. The resulting embryos are implanted in a female of the same or a closely related species. These assisted reproduction techniques have been used with many different species, including African bongo antelopes, gaurs (wild oxen), and wildcats from India and Africa.

Seeing Double

Since 1996, when scientists in Scotland cloned a sheep, cloning has been the subject of intense debate. Cloning is the process of creating an animal that has the same genetic structure as another animal.

To create a clone, scientists collect a skin or tissue cell from a donor animal. The nucleus of this cell contains the DNA of the donor animal. An unfertilized egg is removed from a female of the same species. Scientists then remove the nucleus of the egg

< Black-footed ferrets were first reintroduced into the wild in 1991 in Wyoming.

cell and replace it with the nucleus from the cell of the donor animal. The two cell parts are fused together. The egg now has the donor animal's DNA. Scientists force the cells in the egg to divide, forming an embryo. The embryo is implanted in a surrogate mother, another female who will carry the baby, a few days later. After a full-term pregnancy, the clone—a genetic copy of the donor animal—is born.

Some people view cloning as a way to protect endangered animals. They say that increasing the population of an endangered species through cloning could prevent extinction. Others believe that conservation efforts, such as preserving the habitat of endangered species, should take priority. They fear that people will think there is no need to protect animals if they can be cloned later. Critics also point out the senselessness of cloning

A Zoo Without Elephants?

Can you imagine going to the zoo and not seeing an elephant? That is what might happen over the next few decades if scientists cannot solve a very important mystery. For some reason, elephants in zoos rarely breed. In some cases, male and female elephants at a particular zoo are not compatible. Yet it is difficult to move these enormous animals from one zoo to another to make better matches. In addition, males can be very dangerous or destructive during breeding periods.

Artificial insemination has improved the birthrate of elephants, but problems still remain. Most puzzling to scientists is the fact that many female elephants in zoos do not have normal reproductive cycles. Females without normal cycles cannot conceive at all.

Scientists at the National Zoo are investigating this puzzle. Their research suggests that the social structure of the zoo herds may contribute to the problem. In the wild, the largest and oldest females are in charge of the herd. These elephants usually do not reproduce. Because zoos have limited space, the "herds" are much smaller. A greater percentage of the females have abnormal cycles.

Some zoos are considering the creation of breeding herds that more closely resemble those in the wild. At the same time, researchers are expanding their study of elephant reproductive cycles in the wild. The knowledge gained may help them solve the mystery of elephant reproduction.

∧ A female elephant and her offspring find some shade to get relief from the hot African sun.

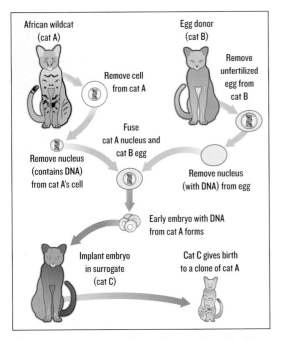

African wildcat
(cat A)

Egg donor
(cat B)

Remove cell
from cat A

Remove
unfertilized
egg from
cat B

Fuse
cat A nucleus and
cat B egg

Remove nucleus
(contains DNA)
from cat A's cell

Remove nucleus
(with DNA) from egg

Early embryo with DNA
from cat A forms

Implant embryo
in surrogate
(cat C)

Cat C gives birth
to a clone of cat A

∧ A cloned animal is the result of fusing cells from different specimens and embedding the resulting embryo in a surrogate.

Seventeen months later, scientists cloned Jazz to produce a wildcat named Ditteaux (pronounced "ditto!"). In 2005, the center announced that Ditteaux had bred naturally with two unrelated, cloned, female wildcats to produce two litters of kittens. Although African wildcats are not endangered, the research that has been done in cloning them can be applied to other cats that are at risk.

∨ Dr. Betsy Dresser and Ditteaux, her African wildcat

endangered animals if there is not a safe place for them to live.

Copy Cats

Dr. Betsy Dresser, director of the Audubon Center for Research of Endangered Species, is an outspoken advocate of the use of cloning as one of many tools to protect endangered species. As she puts it, "Wouldn't it be awful if the habitat was saved, and everyone turned around and said, but where are the animals?"

In 2002, she led a team that froze an African wildcat embryo. The embryo was later thawed and transplanted into a domestic cat. A male kitten named Jazz was born.

Determined Detectives

CHAPTER 5

The Need for Balance

In a remote area of southern Ecuador, clouds embrace the high peaks of the Andes Mountains. Although the area sits near the equator, the region is cold due to the high elevation. The moisture in the thick clouds condenses on the leaves of trees and flowers, dripping onto the ground below. Crystal clear streams carve a path through the pristine cloud forest.

As evening falls, a group of scientists and students adjust headlamps and fasten coats, hoping to guard against the damp cold that seems to seep into their bones. They set out in the darkness, trekking up the mountainside in search of amphibians. Following alpaca trails that wind

< Dr. Joe Mendelson, a herpetologist with Zoo Atlanta, works with Amphibian Ark, an international conservation partnership seeking to save amphibious species that can no longer survive in the wild.

through the forest and paramo (tropical) grasslands, they inspect the vegetation for frogs and toads. One team veers off, following a creek that intersects the trail. Walking slowly up the creek, crouching to look at each leaf and rock, team members periodically reach out to capture an amphibian. The animal is carefully placed in a plastic bag with a little moisture. It will be carried back to camp for further study.

The survey team—led by Dr. Joe Mendelson, a herpetologist at Zoo Atlanta and Martin Bustamante, from Universidad Pontificia Catolica de Ecuador—is in Ecuador to document the diversity of amphibians living in the Mazar Reserve. After a month of searching, the team located nine species of amphibians, five of which were new to science. The most shocking discovery, however, was what the scientists didn't find: No tree frogs. No toads. No glass frogs. Dr. Mendelson's frustration is evident when he says, "Here we are in 2007, still trying to document diversity, and we're too late. They're already extinct."

Dr. Mendelson and Bustamante talked to people living in the area. They described several types of frogs and toads that used to be plentiful in the cloud forest. Then, they said, about ten years ago the creatures just died. Dr. Mendelson suspects that the chytrid fungus is to blame for the deaths.

Λ The marsupial frog, featuring spiky horns over its eyes, is just one species of frog threatened by the chytrid fungus.

Calling All Amphibians!

The release of the Global Amphibian Assessment (GAA) in 2004 represented the first time that all amphibian species known to science had been analyzed in order to figure out their conservation status and distribution around the world. The GAA is an ongoing project, and the information is constantly updated. Almost 600 experts from over 60 countries have so far contributed to the assessment. The study's results are already being used to design strategies to save the world's rapidly declining amphibian populations.

Among the key findings of the GAA:

- Nearly one-third (32%) of the world's amphibian species are threatened, representing 1,896 species. By comparison, just 12% of all bird species and 23% of all mammal species are threatened.

- As many as 165 amphibian species may already be extinct. At least 34 amphibian species are known to be extinct, one is extinct in the wild, while at least another 130 species have not been found in recent years and are possibly extinct.

- At least 43% of all species are declining in population, indicating that the number of threatened species can be expected to rise in the future. In contrast, fewer than one percent of species show population increases.

Source: Global Amphibian Assessment

> **The web-footed coqui (E. karlschmidti) was last observed in Puerto Rico in 1974. It is now believed to be extinct.**

Fungus Fighters

The chytrid fungus is a ruthless killer. Its victims are amphibians— frogs, toads, salamanders, and newts. It has attacked amphibians on every continent except Antarctica, where amphibians do not live. Scientists believe that the fungus is responsible for the extinction of more than 100 species of amphibians since 1980. Nearly 2,000 other species are threatened because of the fungus.

Scientists worldwide have been tracking down the killer since the late 1970s, when frog populations began declining. Tissues from frogs that had died mysteriously were examined under light and electron microscopes. In 1995, Dr. Lee Berger, a veterinarian and then a Ph.D. student at the Australian Animal Health Laboratory, noticed a strange organism that appeared in the tissues. Berger soon isolated the organism and showed that it was sickening amphibians, but the organism remained unidentified. She collaborated with Dr. Peter Daszak, an expert on parasites, and Dr. Louise Goggin, who analyzed the gene sequence. In 1998, the organism was finally identified as a chytrid fungus.

Clues to the Cause

Once scientists determined what was killing the amphibians, other mysteries waited to be solved. Where did the fungus originate? How did it spread to so many continents? A group of researchers at James Cook University in Australia, led by Dr. Rick Speare, sought to find answers.

∧ Mountain yellow-legged frogs photographed at Kings Canyon National Park in California's Sierra Nevada range. The species is facing extinction, which affects the fragile ecosystem of the alpine region.

∨ Researchers Vance Vredenburg and Tate Tunstall of the University of California at Berkeley have spent more than seven years collecting data illustrating the decline in the population of mountain yellow-legged frogs in the Sierra Nevada region. Once the most popular inhabitant, the frogs are endangered by trout populations, fungus, and habitat destruction.

Looking for a Cure

Lurking just under the surface of the water, a saltwater crocodile waits for its prey. When an unwary wallaby approaches the water's edge, the crocodile lunges. Its powerful jaws close around the victim. The crocodile pulls the wallaby beneath the water and holds it there until it drowns.

Saltwater crocodiles, native to northern Australia and Southeast Asia, are the largest reptiles on Earth. Males can grow as long as 23 feet (5 m), tipping the scales at 2,200 pounds (1,000 kg). Given their reputation as man-eaters, it is not surprising that many people do not care whether these aggressive crocodiles or their habitats are protected.

Saltwater crocodiles, however, may someday be the source of powerful new antibiotics. In 2000, a film producer noticed that saltwater crocodiles often fought, tearing off each other's legs or otherwise seriously injuring each other. Despite living in water full of bacteria, the wounds did not get infected. Researchers were later able to identify a substance, which they called crocodillin, in the crocs' blood that kills bacteria, viruses, and fungi.

American alligators, once endangered but now making a comeback, are also resistant to infections. Dr. Mark Merchant at McNeese State University in Louisiana discovered proteins in alligator blood that kill life-threatening bacteria and viruses, such as HIV and E. coli. More research remains to be done, but Merchant and other researchers hope to use these crocodile and alligator proteins to develop medicines that can destroy today's deadly diseases.

^ Saltwater crocodiles are difficult to study. Dangerous to humans, they can grow up to 20 feet (6 m) long.

The team knew that the fungus had been identified in frog populations in South Africa. They also knew that African clawed frogs had been exported to countries in Europe and North America as well as to Australia and New Zealand. The scientists decided to investigate further.

They traveled to five African museums where nearly 700 clawed frogs had been collected and preserved between 1879 and 1999. They conducted tests on a small piece of tissue from each frog. The earliest evidence of the chytrid fungus was on a frog captured in 1938. The scientists also determined that infected frogs were found throughout southern Africa by 1973. However, the clawed frogs had not shown any signs of disease in the wild. Based on this evidence, Dr. Speare and his team believe that the chytrid fungus originated in Africa.

Unbalanced Habitats

Different locations, such as deserts and tropical rain forests, have different types of plants and animals living in them. In each of these ecosystems, the plants and animals have developed a balance that allows all of them to survive. But sometimes a plant or animal from

⋀ The population of the Corroboree frog, native to Australia, has plummeted to less than 200 as a result of the chytrid fungus, which attacks the frog's skin and eventually suffocates the amphibian.

another location is introduced into an ecosystem. Often, the new plant or animal has no natural enemies in its new home. It can take over the ecosystem, upsetting the normal balance. It can also introduce diseases into the area. Either action can cause a great deal of damage, even the extinction of native plants or animals.

In the late 1800s, some American gardeners began growing a sweet-smelling, flowering Japanese vine called kudzu. The fast-growing vine was promoted as a way to control erosion (the wearing away of earth) in the 1930s and 1940s. Today, the plant grows out of control in many parts of the southeastern United States. As it climbs and covers native trees, they die from lack of sunlight.

Researchers suspect the chytrid fungus was introduced accidentally when, in the 1930s, scientists developed a pregnancy test using frogs. Because the African clawed frogs were easy to care for in a lab setting, there was a large demand for them. The frogs, carrying the

⋀ The kudzu vine has taken over forestland throughout the southeastern United States. It is a classic example of an invasive species taking over native ecosystems.

∧ A healthy yellow-legged frog at Milestone Basin in California's Sierra Nevada range. Hundreds of this species of frog in the region died from the chytrid fungus during the summer of 2005.

chytrid fungus, were shipped around the world. Over time, some frogs may have escaped from the labs. When they reached a stream or lake, the fungus was introduced into a new ecosystem.

Although scientists have identified the chytrid fungus, it is still killing amphibians. Around the world, scientists are working in labs, racing against time to save dwindling amphibian populations. Some scientists are developing and testing antifungal drugs. Others are working on diagnostic tests that can be conducted in the field, allowing biologists to confirm the presence of the chytrid fungus in an area within days, instead of weeks or months.

In 2007, a team of researchers led by Dr. Jess Morgan of the University of California, Berkeley, and the Department of Primary Industries and Fisheries in

Queensland, Australia, discovered that the fungus may be able to produce spores that can live in an environment for a decade. This is especially dangerous because the chytrid fungus does not kill frogs right away. They may move to new areas before they die, spreading the fungus with them through the water or on land. Those spores could also be carried to a new location by birds or on the soles of shoes, making the fungus harder to destroy. Researchers are now trying to determine where the spores live.

Environmental groups and park agencies are taking precautions to warn people what to do if they come in contact with amphibians. Warnings against moving frogs from one place to another and cleaning footwear and vehicle tires are some of the safety measures visitors to these habitats are asked to take.

CHAPTER 6

A View From Above

Looking Beneath the Surface

A research vessel belonging to the Planetary Coral Reef Foundation cuts through the Pacific Ocean just south of the equator. Ahead are the Phoenix Islands, a group of eight remote islands. One of the islands is inhabited. Its nearest neighbors are 600 miles (966 km) away. The ship anchors a mile offshore to avoid damaging the reefs surrounding the islands. A Zodiac is lowered into the ocean. Diving teams will use the small boat as a base from which to explore the reefs.

Excitement is high as the Zodiac nears one of the islands. An expedition from the New England

< Branches of coral hide a variety of fish. Many species of fish find safety from predators and a plentiful food source in a coral reef.

Λ Divers from the Mote Marine Laboratory measure and record data on coral in the waters off Summerland Key, Florida. The state is funding a study to analyze traumatized coral reefs off the coast in order to prevent a repeat of a mass bleaching in 1990 that killed off more than 30 percent of the coral in the region.

Aquarium, visiting the islands two years earlier, in 2002, had reported a vibrant coral reef habitat, undisturbed by humans. Now the divers will have the chance to check the health of the reef and see its beauty for themselves.

The Zodiac hovers over the reef, gently rocking in the ocean's swells. The divers adjust their scuba gear and prepare to roll over the side of the boat. Suddenly, they see long, dark shapes slicing through the water toward the boat. Sharks!

One diver eases into the water to test their reaction. The sharks are curious, but not aggressive, so the other divers grab their equipment and roll backward into the water. Armed with underwater writing tablets and digital video cameras, the divers swim toward the reef. Sharks, red snappers, parrotfish, and barracudas swirl around the divers, flashes of color in the clear sea.

V Divers researching coral reefs often see sharks and other marine wildlife.

Looking past the fish, the divers get their first look at the reef itself. They stop in shock and dismay. Expecting to find a rainbow of yellow, green, and purple corals, they find devastation. Only skeletons of the once vibrant corals remain, covered by destructive algae. What had happened?

Rain Forests of the Sea

Coral reefs are among the most beautiful ecosystems in the world. The corals, themselves marine animals, provide the foundation for a rich, underwater world. Within their tissues they shelter one-celled algae called zooxanthalle—these plants provide the energy the corals need to build their skeletons as well as give them their color. When they die, hard corals leave behind their skeletons. Over time, these rock-like structures grow, cemented together by tiny invertebrates and plants. Soft corals,

∧ A healthy coral reef is home to thousands of species of plants and animals.

Biodiversity

One measure of the health of an ecosystem is its biological diversity—the number of different plants and animals sharing the ecosystem. These plants and animals rely on each other for survival. A healthy ecosystem is able to protect itself and recover from threats, whether natural or caused by humans. When one population within the ecosystem is in danger, however, others are threatened as well. For example, many species of fish eat the algae that grow on corals. When too many fish are caught, the algae grow unchecked, choking the corals. When the corals die, the entire ecosystem can collapse.

∧ Bioerosion, naturally occurring erosion caused by plants and animals, leaves coral brittle and vulnerable to collapse.

sponges, anemones, and sea urchins make their home in the hard coral reef, as do small animals such as shrimp and fish. The teeming life found in a healthy reef community draws predators such as sharks and eels. Known for their biodiversity, coral reefs have been called "the rain forests of the sea."

Built up over thousands of years, coral reefs are home to over one-fourth of all fish species. Reefs are a growing source of tourism income for developing countries. Reefs are also vital to the safety of coastal regions, protecting these areas from waves and storms. People have not protected the reefs, however. As a result, many of the world's coral reefs are in crisis.

One of the gravest dangers to coral reefs is global warming. As the Earth's climate changes, sea temperatures are rising. In 1998, sea surface temperatures rose well above average, bleaching corals around the world. When bleaching occurs, corals get stressed and lose the microscopic plants that live in their top layer. Without the colors from the plants, the corals turn white. Although bleached corals often die, they can recover if they are not too severely damaged. However, once they die, it may take five to ten years for corals to colonize the area again.

The researchers at the Phoenix Islands noted that water temperatures in 2002 were above average for three months. Given the remoteness of the islands and the few humans who live there, other common threats to coral reefs such as pollution, erosion due to coastal development, and overfishing were ruled out. The researchers believe that bleaching caused by unusually high ocean temperatures destroyed the once vibrant coral reef communities.

Eye in the Sky

Concern for coral reefs began to grow in the early 1990s. Scientists and divers knew that reefs in some parts of the world were stressed, but there were no baseline data with which to monitor changes. There was not even a map showing the location of all the world's reefs. The Millennium Coral Reef Mapping Project, a cooperative effort of U.S. government agencies, international groups, and universities, set out to get some much needed information.

Coral Reef Fast Facts

■ 20 percent of the world's coral reefs have been destroyed, with no sign of recovery.

■ 67 percent of the world's reefs are at serious risk of dying.

■ 16 percent of the world's reefs were seriously damaged in 1998 when waters were much warmer than usual. Less than half have recovered.

■ 24 percent of the world's reefs are at immediate risk from human pressures, including destructive fishing practices, poor land management of coastal regions, and increased pollution. Another 26 percent are at increased risk in the long term.

■ Reefs in the Caribbean have lost up to 80 percent of their coral cover. There are some signs of recovery.

▼ A reef under stress will lose the algae that give the coral its diverse colors, resulting in a bleaching effect. In this photograph, the healthy coral is purple, while the dying coral is slowly bleaching to a murky whitish color.

Traditionally, scientists had to travel around the world on research vessels in order to gather data on reefs and map their locations. This method is both expensive and time-consuming. Instead, the Millennium Project scientists looked to space to solve these problems. There, 438 miles (705 km) above Earth's surface, the LandSat 7 satellite orbits the planet. It completes an orbit every 99 minutes, collecting data about Earth's surface. Every 16 days, it covers the entire Earth, acquiring data for up to 4,000 locations. This information is downloaded to computers on Earth, where it is translated into images.

∧ A view of the LandSat 7 satellite in space

Beginning in 1999, scientists worked with LandSat managers to make sure that the satellite captured images of all reef areas during its orbits. Then a map was created using the 1,490 satellite images that were gathered. Today, these images are used by scientists and others to monitor the world's reefs.

∨ The Phoenix Islands saw massive bleaching of their coral reefs, but many coral, like the table coral pictured, were able to survive quite well. Recovery is proceeding more quickly in areas where conservation efforts are taking place, confirming that action is needed to help protect and maintain the survival of many of these ocean species.

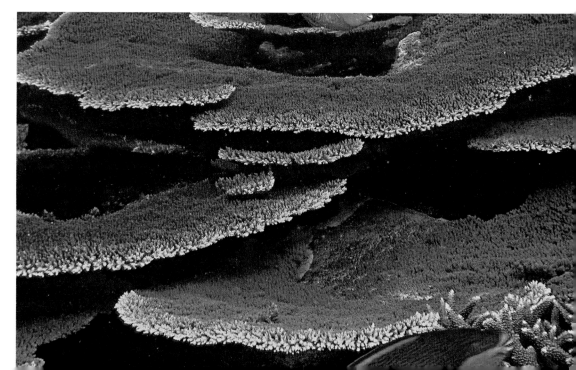

Truth on the Ground

Satellite images are not like photographs. Images of coral reefs can be particularly challenging to interpret since they are under water. As a result, scientists conduct ground truthing of the satellite images to learn how to interpret the images. Ground truthing matches observations and data collections taken on the ground with the satellite images that were taken at the same time. Once scientists know how a particular reef appears in a satellite image, they can identify those same conditions or features in other images.

The Planetary Coral Reef Foundation, among other organizations, has been conducting ground truthing of satellite images in the Southeast Asia Sea. Diving crews collect field data, recording images of each coral reef community. The divers inventory the different species of coral and record their health and location. Once the crews are back aboard the research vessel, the information is entered into a computer.

The information the field researchers gather enables them to interpret the colors in the satellite images accurately. They learn which colors show sand flats and which represent beds of sea grass, which colors represent healthy corals and which show dying communities. Once these correlations are made, the information can be used to interpret other images.

In 2006, the Millennium Coral Reef Mapping project recorded its findings in the first complete survey of its kind and published its report in an international scientific journal. Sadly, the study concluded that less than 2 percent of coral reefs around the world are in areas that are protected from human activities which harm them. Additionally, although the amount of marine areas under protection has increased in recent years, the majority of coral reefs within those regions, and the wildlife that lives among them, are not properly protected.

∧ A coral reef, like rain forests throughout the world, is host to an enormous variety of wildlife, making it one of the most diverse ecosystems on the planet.

Signs of Hope

∧ A bald eagle flies over Lake Coeur d'Alene in Idaho. Although delisted as an endangered species in 2007, the bald eagle is still protected from "disturbance" by the federal Bald and Golden Eagle Protection Act.

High overhead, a bald eagle soars on a column of warm air. Best known as a symbol of the United States, it also symbolizes a success for the Endangered Species Act. Grizzly bears and gray wolves once again roam Yellowstone National Park, and the red wolf is making a slow comeback in North Carolina. Golden lion tamarins chatter and climb through the forests of Brazil. Pods of gray whales glide through the cold waters of the North Pacific.

Despite these and other success stories, destruction of habitat and hunting around the globe continue to threaten the very existence of many animals. Their future is not without hope, however. Scientists, conservation groups, many governments, and individuals around the world continue to work tirelessly on their behalf.

International conservation organizations such as WWF (World Wildlife Fund) and the Wildlife Conservation Society work with governments, communities, and scientists to promote conservation and maintain protected reserves. Other groups, such as the Sierra Club, Friends of the Earth, and the Rainforest Action Network, involve communities in local conservation projects. They act as watchdogs, alerting the public to development projects that threaten the environment and organizing campaigns against corporations and governments that contribute to deforestation. Together, scientists and other committed individuals are working to save Earth's endangered animals. The changes they accomplish may someday protect the existence of humans as well. What will you do to help?

Glossary

bioacoustics — the science of studying the sounds animals make and how animals react to the sounds around them

biodiversity — biological diversity in an ecosystem, shown by the number of different plants and animals that live there

black market — the business of buying or selling illegal goods

bushmeat — meat from wild animals that are often on the endangered list

census survey — a count of the population of a particular species

circa — about; used to indicate a date that is approximate

clone — a genetic copy of an animal; to produce an animal that is a genetic copy of another

conserve — to maintain or preserve the population of an endangered species

delisted — removed from the endangered species list

ecosystem — a community of organisms together with their physical environment

endangered species — plants and animals that are in immediate danger of becoming extinct

genetic diversity — genetic variation within a population

global warming — an increase in Earth's average temperature that causes environmental change

ground truthing — collecting information at a location at the same time that a remote sensing system, such as a satellite, is gathering data; using such information to interpret satellite images

habitat — the environment in which a plant or animal lives

inbreeding — the breeding of individual animals that are closely related to each other

nocturnal — active at night

scat — animal droppings

species — an animal population that shares common traits; a biological classification

spectrogram — a picture of a sound that shows its volume, pitch, and frequency

◁ An adult male black-footed ferret at the National Black-footed Ferret Conservation Center in Wyoming

Bibliography

Books

McGavin, George C. *Endangered: Wildlife on the Brink of Extinction.* Buffalo, NY: Firefly Books, 2006.

Miles, Victoria. *Wild Science: Amazing Encounters Between Animals and the People Who Study Them.* Vancouver: Raincoast Books, 2004.

Swinburne, Stephen R. *Once a Wolf: How Wildlife Biologists Fought to Bring Back the Gray Wolf.* Boston: Houghton Mifflin, 1999.

Articles

Stone, Gregory S. "Phoenix Islands: a Coral Reef Wilderness Revealed." NATIONAL GEOGRAPHIC (February 2004): 48–65.

On the Web

Audubon Center for Research of Endangered Species
http://www.auduboninstitute.org/sitePage
Server?pagename=Facility_Research_Center

Census of Marine Life
http://www.coml.org/

The Consortium for the Barcode of Life
http://www.barcoding.si.edu/

The Elephant Listening Project
http://www.birds.cornell.edu/brp/elephant/

> The humpback whale, found in oceans throughout the world, is currently on the endangered species list.

Planetary Coral Reef Foundation
http://www.pcrf.org/

Polar Bears International
http://www.polarbearsinternational.org/

San Diego Zoo Center for Conservation and Research for Endangered Species
http://cres.sandiegozoo.org/

Further Reading

Collet, Anne. *Swimming with Giants: My Encounters with Whales, Dolphins, and Seals.* Minneapolis, MN: Milkweed Editions, 2000.

Patent, Dorothy Hinshaw. *Biodiversity.* Boston, MA: Clarion Books, 1996.

Poole, Joyce. *Elephants (World Life Library).* Stillwater, MN: Voyageur Press, 1997.

Rosing, Norbert. *Face to Face with Polar Bears.* Washington, D.C.: National Geographic, 2007.

Tocci, Salvatore. *Coral Reefs: Life Below the Sea.* New York: Franklin Watts, 2005.

Index

Boldface indicates illustrations.

About the Author

Sandra Pobst has 20 years experience in the educational field, writing books on science and social-studies topics for middle-schoolers, developing educational software, and creating curriculum materials for elementary schools. A former elementary school teacher, Pobst enjoys the opportunity to make recent scientific discoveries accessible to young people. She holds a Bachelor of Science degree in Elementary Education from Kansas State University. She lives with her husband and two children in Austin, Texas.

Consultant

As a professor of wildlife conservation at the University of Massachusetts, Amherst, Todd Fuller delights in teaching and working with students studying the natural history and ecology of large mammals throughout the world. He is especially interested in figuring out how wildlife populations get bigger or smaller, and thus how to make sure none go extinct. Fuller lives with his wife, a forester, and his daughter, a 5th grader, on a small farm in western Massachusetts.

Λ One species of prairie dog in Utah is endangered due to habitat loss and poisoning programs by ranchers whose cattle compete with the prairie dog for grass. Other animals including the black-footed ferret are endangered because there are fewer prairie dogs for them to prey upon.

Founded in 1888, the National Geographic Society is one of the largest nonprofit scientific and educational organizations in the world. It reaches more than 285 million people worldwide each month through its official journal, NATIONAL GEOGRAPHIC, and its four other magazines; the National Geographic Channel; television documentaries; radio programs; films; books; videos and DVDs; maps; and interactive media. National Geographic has funded more than 8,000 scientific research projects and supports an education program combating geographic illiteracy.

For more information, please call 1–800–NGS LINE (647–5463) or write to the following address:

National Geographic Society
1145 17th Street N.W., Washington, D.C.
20036-4688 U.S.A.

Visit us online at
www.nationalgeographic.com/books

For librarians and teachers:
www.ngchildrensbooks.com

More for kids from National Geographic:
kids.nationalgeographic.com

For information about special discounts for bulk purchases, please contact: National Geographic Books Special Sales: ngspecsales@ngs.org

For rights or permissions inquiries, please contact National Geographic Books Subsidiary Rights: ngbookrights@ngs.org

Library of Congress Cataloging-in-Publication Data available upon request

Hardcover ISBN: 978-1-4263-0358-6

Library ISBN: 978-1-4263-0265-7

Printed in China

Book design by Dan Banks, Project Design Company

**Published by the
National Geographic Society**
John M. Fahey, Jr., *President and Chief Executive Officer;* Gilbert M. Grosvenor, *Chairman of the Board;* Tim T. Kelly, *President, Global Media Group;* Nina D. Hoffman, *Executive Vice President; President, Book Publishing Group*

Prepared by the Book Division
Nancy Laties Feresten, *Vice President, Editor in Chief, Children's Books;* Bea Jackson, *Director of Design and Illustrations, Children's Books;* Amy Shields, *Executive Editor, Series, Children's Books*

Staff for This Book
Virginia Ann Koeth, *Editor*
Jim Hiscott, *Art Director*
Lori Epstein, *Illustrations Editor*
Lewis R. Bassford, *Production Manager*
Stuart Armstrong, *Graphics*

Martin Walz, *Maps*
Grace Hill, *Associate Managing Editor*
Jennifer A. Thornton, *Managing Editor*
R. Gary Colbert, *Production Director*
Susan Borke, *Legal and Business Affairs*

Manufacturing and Quality Management
Christopher A. Liedel, *Chief Financial Officer*
Phillip L. Schlosser, *Vice President*
Chris Brown, *Technical Director*
Nicole Elliott, *Manager*

A Creative Media Applications, Inc. Production
Editor: Susan Madoff
Copy Editor: Lauire Lieb
Design and Production: Luís Leon and Fabia Wargin